Row the Boat

John 21:1–11
(Jesus Fills the Nets)

by Mary Manz Simon
Illustrated by Dennis Jones

CONCORDIA PUBLISHING HOUSE • SAINT LOUIS

Books by Mary Manz Simon from Concordia Publishing House

Hear Me Read Level 1 Series
(also available in Spanish)
- Bing!
- Come to Jesus
- Drip Drop
- Follow That Star
- Hide the Baby
- Hurry, Hurry!
- Jibber Jabber
- Row the Boat
- Rumble, Rumble
- Send a Baby
- A Silent Night
- Sit Down
- Too Tall, Too Small
- Toot! Toot!
- What Next?
- Where Is Jesus?
- Who Will Help?
- Whoops!

Little Visits Series
- Little Visits Every Day
- Little Visits for Families
- Little Visits for Toddlers

Hear Me Read Level 2 Series
- Daniel & the Tattletales
- The First Christmas
- The Hide-and-Seek Prince
- Hurray for the Lord's Army
- The No-Go King
- Thank You Jesus
- Through the Roof
- Walk on the Waves

Hear Me Read Big Books
- Follow That Star
- Send a Baby
- Sit Down*
- Too Tall, Too Small
- What Next?
- Where Is Jesus?*
- Who Will Help?*

* also available in Classroom Sets

God's Children Pray

Copyright © 1990 Concordia Publishing House
3558 S. Jefferson Avenue, St. Louis, MO 63118-3968
Manufactured in Colombia

All rights reserved. No part of this publication may be reproduced, stored in a retrieval system, or transmitted, in any form or by any means, electronic, mechanical, photocopying, recording, or otherwise, without the prior written permission of Concordia Publishing House.

07 08 09 10 11 12 13 14 15   12 11 10 09 08 07 06 05 04

HEAR·ME·READ

Name

Date

Presented by

To the Adult:

Early readers need two kinds of reading: they need to be read to, and they need to do their own reading. The Hear Me Read Bible Stories series helps you to encourage your child with both kinds.

For example, your child might read this book as you sit together. Listen attentively. Assist gently, if needed. Encourage, be patient, and be positive about your child's efforts.

Then perhaps you'd like to share this Bible story in an easy-to-understand translation or paraphrase.

Using both types of reading gives your child a chance to develop new skills and pride in reading. You share and support your child's excitement.

As a mother and a teacher, I anticipate the joy your child will feel in saying, "Hear me read Bible stories!"

Mary Manz Simon

For Hank
1 John 4:10–12

"Let's go fishing," said the man.

"Let's row the boat,"
said the man.

Row, row, row the boat.

"Let's fish here," said the man.
"Put the net down.
Put the net down here."

"No fish!" said the man.

"Look. There are no fish.

There are no fish in the net."

Row, row, row the boat.

"Let's fish here," said the man.
"Put the net down.
Put the net down here."

"No fish!" said the man.

"Look.

There are no fish.

There are no fish in the net."

"Look," said the man.

"Look at the fish."

Row, row, row the boat.

"Put the net down," said the man.
"Put the net down here."

"No fish!" said the man.

"Look.

There are no fish.

There are no fish in the net."

Jesus said, "Go fishing here."

Row, row, row the boat.

Jesus said, "Put the net down."

"Put the net down here."

"Look!" said the man.
"Look at the fish."

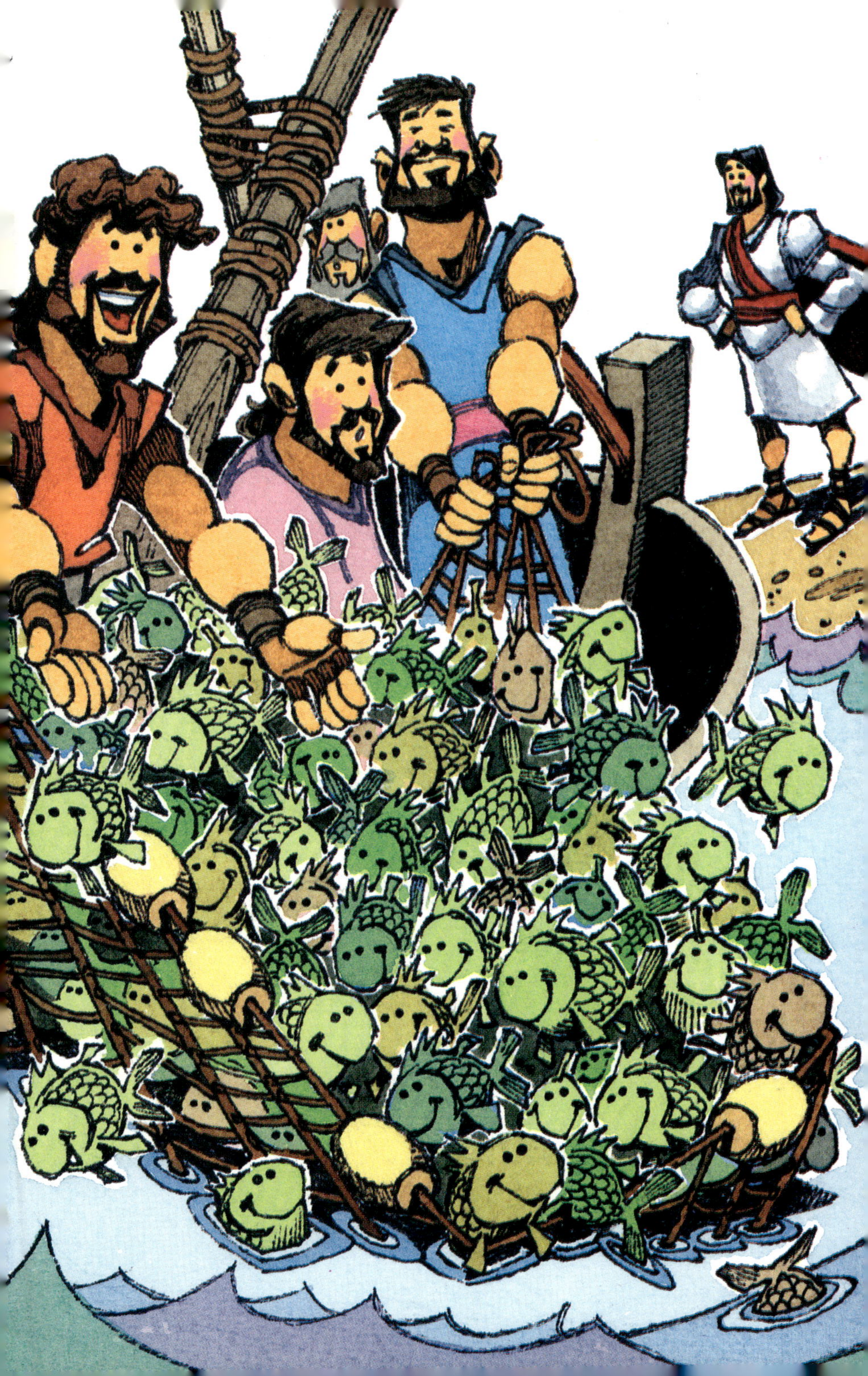

About the Author

Mary Manz Simon holds a doctoral degree in education with a specialty in early childhood education. She has taught at levels from preschool through postgraduate. Dr. Simon is the best-selling author of more than 30 children's books, including *Little Visits with Jesus.* She and her husband, the Reverend Henry A. Simon, are the parents of three children.